TEACH YOUR TODDLER TO READ THROUGH PLAY

A Detailed Account with over 130
Game/Activities Tips, and Resources

ANDREA STEPHENSON

Copyright © 2019 by Andrea Stephenson

All rights reserved. No part of this book may be used or reproduced by any means, graphic, electronic, or mechanical, including photocopying, recording, taping, or by any information storage retrieval system, without the written permission of the publisher except in the case of brief quotations embodied in critical articles and reviews.

DEDICATION

To my son Cory,

Thank you for being the inspiration behind what I write, read, and research. Your presence has encouraged me to pursue my dreams so I can be a constant support for you. Your curiosity and outgoing personality have pushed me in ways I couldn't have imagined. You have made me a better person. I thank God for you.

I love you,

Mom

REVIEWS

"This was a wonderfully detailed account of not only how to teach your child to read, but also how to connect with your child, support your child in a lifetime of loving to learn, and use your time caring for your child in a meaningful, fulfilling way. I am inspired as a mother, and I wish I'd known about this sooner!I thought it was very well written, and the flow was perfect. The book flowed seamlessly from one chapter to the next, and I felt like it was organized perfectly."

-Stacey Kopp

"This is a wonderful guidebook for parents who want to help their children begin learning at an early age through play. It is an introduction on how to nurture a love of learning and proficiency in reading in children, which in turn will open the door for your child to be exposed to and learn about a variety of topics. Andrea incorporates several learning styles in order to pave the way for a lifetime of learning.

I look forward to incorporating some of these techniques into playtime with my little learners."

-Danielle J.

"This book documents the journey of an engaged parent who used creative and fun ways to introduce her son to books. This led to the child's continuous interest in letters, words, sentences and naturally, reading. If you are willing to invest the time in incorporating the tips in this book with your child, he or she will also develop an interest in books and learn to read during the early stages of brain development. This book is an excellent example of the African Proverb "Each One Teach One."

-Linsey Mills

ABOUT ME

Hello, and thank you for purchasing my book! My name is Andrea Stephenson, and I am a wife and the mommy of a curious, energetic three-year-old boy!

I am a Licensed Clinical Social Worker who created the organization Simply Outrageous Youth (SOY). SOY was created because of the need to teach our children life skills using fun and hands-on methods.

When I was young, my family used games, role play, and real-life experiences to teach me various life lessons. For example, my older brother taught me about credit and the stock market through a game he created called *Traders*.

Once I became a mom, I wanted to create these same experiences for my son and children around the world.

I have done extensive research on how kids' brains develop and how to engage them in fun learning methods even as babies.

When my son was born I constantly played and interacted with him to create a strong bond. I saw how much he loved learning. This interaction coupled with my research resulted in him learning to talk in full sentences at nineteen months and read at twenty-one months.

This book was written to show you exactly how this was done without worksheets and flashcards. It was all done through **play**!

Believe me, it was not my intention to teach him how to read at such an early age. I didn't think he would learn the alphabet until three or four-years-old.

I followed my child's lead in him wanting to absorb more knowledge, and I used the social worker mantra when dealing with others, which is, "Meet them where they are."

You will see that I used the same activities to teach my child various aspects of reading. For example, singing and dancing were used to teach my son the alphabet and as a tool to introduce him to new words.

My purpose is to open your eyes to a new way of learning. Learning can take place anywhere. Just think of our planet as a big learning playground.

Let's start this fun adventure together!

ANDREA STEPHENSON

www.SimplyOutrageousYouth.org

AMills@SimplyOutrageousYouth.com

Follow me on:

www.pinterest.com/SimplyOutrageousYouth

https://www.youtube.com/channel/UCsGkzT_Wndiq8SEOttmB4Ag

Table of Contents

Chapter 1: What Do You Mean Your 21-Month-Old Son Could Read?..................1

Chapter 2: The Beginning..................7

Chapter 3: Familiarity with Language 18

Chapter 4: In-Depth Learning 30

Chapter 5: Learning the Alphabet 43

Chapter 6: Phonics..................52

Chapter 7: Blending Sounds..................58

Chapter 8: Sight Words 65

Chapter 9: Experience 75

Chapter 10: Digital Media 87

Chapter 11: Reading a Variety of Books..................98

Chapter 12: Structuring Your Day and Game Plan 109

Chapter 13: Tips for When a Child Loses Interest in Reading......116

Chapter 14: What We Do Now 124

Sight Word List..................136

CHAPTER 1

What Do You Mean Your 21-Month-Old Son Could Read?

YOUR 21-MONTH-OLD SON COULD READ? WHAT DOES THAT MEAN?

People Were Shocked!

There were many occasions when my son, Cory, and I were in a store or library, and he would read signs or book titles. The person near us would look and ask, "How old is he?" I replied by saying he was a one-year-old but would be two very soon. You could see their brains turning trying to figure out how this baby could read. They would then ask if he had seen the sign or read the book before. I told them, "No."

The next question would be, "How is he reading as a one-year-old?" My quick answer was "Through reading books and play." I could have sat down with them and had an hour-long conversation about our process. However, there wasn't enough time.

He Could Read Independently

I did not tell friends that Cory could read. The only people who knew were immediate family. They could not believe it either. They asked, "What do you mean he can read?" They thought he remembered the words from books we read often. He actually did this in the beginning. However, one day I gave him a new book and he started reading it.

I was amazed by this. Then I gave him another book and he started reading that as well. The two books were *Whose Toes Are Those?* by Jabari Asim, and *Baby Happy Baby Sad* by Leslie Patricelli.

In the spring of 2016, my sister-in-law and brother babysat Cory while my husband and I went to a wedding. During the festivities, they sent me videos of him playing and reading pages from two books. Of course, there were some words he struggled with in the video, like *hexagon*. However, he read most of the books independently. If he didn't know a word, he had the ability to sound out three-letter and four-letter words.

Past the Point of Remembering Words

When my son independently read his first word, he knew the phonics and how to blend sounds to make words. We often played the *Word Game*, where we used Cory's magnetic letters to spell words on the refrigerator. One day, I put the letters *M*, *A*, and *T* on the refrigerator and said, "Can you sound out this word?" All of sudden I heard his little voice say, "MMM-AAA-TTT, Mat!"

My husband and I looked at each other in shock. Then I gave him more short *a* words like *pan*, *can*, and *fan*. We continued with short *i*, *e*, *o*, and *u* words. He was able to sound out all the words I gave him.

What Books Could He Read?

I gave my son books that were for babies, toddlers, and preschoolers to read. They were mostly hardcover picture books that were sturdy. These types of books have a lot of three-letter and four-letter words and help children make connections between text and pictures. They also included objects he was familiar with, such as animals, letters, shapes, numbers, and body parts.

Examples of some book titles are *Brown Bear, Brown Bear, What do You See?* by Bill Martin Jr., *Dear Zoo: A Lift-the-Flap Book* by Rod Campbell, and *From Head to Toe* by Eric Carle. These books increased his confidence because he could read most of the words with little help from me.

Books on His Level and Slowly Progressed to More Difficult Ones

Once Cory's confidence began to increase with reading, I *slowly* progressed to books on reading level 1, such as *Max Goes to the Dentist* by Adria R. Klein. These books contain three-letter words, four-letter words, and sight words. At this point, my son would ask me for help if he did not know a word.

Instead of just telling him the word, I would get creative. Sometimes I would act out the word or pretend I did not know it and sound it out like he would. For example, if he did not know the word *jump*, I would jump around the room until he said the word. If he saw the word *push*, I would sound it out by saying, ppp-uuu-shhhh. I explained that *sh* makes the shhh sound.

The purpose of this was to make learning fun and to encourage curiosity. It also demonstrated to my son that he could sound out words just like I did if he did not know them. Furthermore, if he could not figure a word out, I wanted him to learn that asking me a question often resulted in a fun and positive encounter.

Cory reading a list of words in a book at one-year-old.

TIP #1
Teach reading through play.

TIP #2
Start with picture books.

TIP #3
Encourage curiosity.

CHAPTER 2

The Beginning

BONDING WITH MY BABY

How It All Started

While I was three months pregnant, I had lunch with two former co-workers, Cyndi and Teresa. They were overjoyed about my pregnancy, as I had been planning this for over a year. We discussed the joys of motherhood and what to expect. Then Cyndi said something I would remember forever. She said, "You need to start reading to your baby now." I knew that I should talk to my baby while in the womb, but reading to him never crossed my mind.

Cyndi revealed that she just watched Dr. Ben Carson discuss brain health on a PBS special and he emphasized the importance of reading to children. She encouraged me to watch the special on YouTube. I did what she asked, and, boy, was I taken aback by what I learned.

Ben Carson PBS Special

During the special, Dr. Carson said that a baby's brain continues to develop once he/she is born.[1] The more a baby learns, the more the brain's neurons and synapses are making connections.

---

[1] Dr. Ben Carson. "The Missing Link" The Science of Brain Health. PBS. https://www.ket.org/series/MLSB/all/. Accessed 1/14/2019.

Babies who experience interaction with caregivers through songs, cuddling, playing, and talking develop connections in the brain faster and better. By the time a child is three-years-old, their brains have reached 90 percent of their growth. According to Dr. Joann Deak, language centers of the brain are exceptionally responsive in the first three years of life. [2]

Your child is soaking up knowledge at a rapid pace during the first three years of life. I witnessed this first while working as a mobile play therapist with a three-year-old girl who was diagnosed with autism. I observed her playing with the alphabet one day, and she held the *P* and made the "p" sound. I held up more letters and asked her about the various letter sounds. She gave me the correct sound for each letter. Her mom told me she learned the phonics through reading and watching LeapFrog cartoons.

While baby and toddler brains are learning at a rapid pace, not all of the neurons and synapses will remain as the child grows. A child's life experience will activate certain neurons, create new neurons among them, and strengthen existing connections. When certain synaptic pathways are not activated, there is a pruning process which happens, most rapidly during preschool years, and those unused connections are eliminated.

---

[2] JoAnn Deak PhD. "Your Baby's Brain: How Parents Can Help Children Reach Their Potential Brain Power." PBS Kids. http://www.pbs.org/parents/experts/archive/2012/10/your-babys-brain-how-parents-c.html. Accessed 1/14/2019.

How I Applied the Knowledge

These facts fascinated me, and I made three decisions. The first decision was to buy Dr. Ben's DVD series on brain health. My second choice was to go to the library to borrow books and start reading to my little bun in the oven. Lastly, I decided that *play* would be the best way to interact with my son and boost his development once he was born.

Our playtime included activities such as singing, dancing, walking, talking and reading when he was a newborn.

This was the key to my son reading at twenty-one months.

Sing

In the Middle of the Night

I sung constantly to my son. It became one of the tools I used to soothe him and myself in the middle of the night. It can be tiresome as a mom to constantly wake up at night to feed your baby. Singing was a strategy I used to calm myself, and it helped me persevere through the night.

During Car Rides

Singing during car rides is a great way to bond with a baby. Babies love to hear their mother's voices, especially in the tune of a song. I sung toddler songs such as "The Wheels on the Bus" and "Baa Baa Black

Sheep." If my son cried during car rides, singing was a tool that made him stop.

While Feeding and Changing Diapers

Moments where your child is looking and focused on you are great times to sing. During feeding time and diaper changes, my son always looked into my eyes. Many times, he would stop sucking on my breast or bottle and look at me so he could concentrate on what I was singing. Once Cory started to smile, he often moved his feet and arms and grinned during my songs at diaper changes.

Talk

My goal was to talk to my son about various topics. Talking is a great way to interact with a baby. I talked all the time. Sometimes if I ran out of things to say, then I would pick an object in the room and describe it or explain its function. During breakfast and dinner time, I would tell classic stories such as "The Three Little Pigs" or "Goldilocks and the Three Bears." I also created stories about the alphabet and various animals we previously read about in books. During grocery shopping, I identified foods and the letters they started with.

Dancing

Dancing is one of my favorite activities to do, and I wanted my son to join the fun. While Pandora Toddler Radio Station played in the background, I often picked my son up and danced with him. His face became focused as his eyes observed the room while we swayed side to side and around. Cory's favorite song to dance to was "All Aboard the Choo Choo Train" by Choo Choo Soul. When this song came on, he often kicked his legs and held his arm out so I could pick him up to dance.

Holding Your Child

Holding your baby and looking into their eyes is the best way to connect with them. After delivering a baby, doctors usually give moms their babies for skin-to-skin time. The purpose of this activity is for mom and baby to bond. When a mother holds their child, the baby is taking note of their mother's scent and studying her face. This provides a safe space for the child when they are crying and can't self soothe.

Sign Language

Sign Language was the second language my son used to communicate with me besides crying. It is amazing how it allows babies to communicate without speaking. Cory learned simple signs that he needed, such as *all done* (with eating and drinking), *milk*, and *help*. While singing I would sign the words for visual stimulation. My brother sent me an app called Baby Sign Language Dictionary App which teaches you over three hundred signs for your baby. I started signing to my son at three months, and at four months he used the sign for *milk* to tell me he was hungry. Our connection became stronger because my son felt he could communicate his needs to me.

Reading

I read to my son before naptime and bedtime. Holding your child while reading is a great bonding experience. As a baby, Cory liked picture books with colorful images and short sentences. He was able to turn the board book pages by nine months. We began with reading one or two books per day. Then it increased to ten books because he loved hearing me read. These types of books were perfect because they were short and kept his attention. I do not recommend reading long books to babies unless they have built the attention span for it.

Recognizing Books

One day my son and I were playing in the basement. I asked him to get the book *Brown Bear Brown Bear* out of the bin. Out of the twelve books in the bin, he picked the correct title. I was amazed. Then I asked him to get the book *Thank You, God!* by Kathleen Bostrom, and again he brought the correct book to me. This experience taught me that babies have the ability to recognize words if they are exposed to them multiple times.

Going for a walk with baby Cory at six weeks. During our walks, I would describe the animals, colors, and anything we viewed outside. I often continued to talk even as he slept.

ACTIVITIES

The activities below will show you how to use one song to introduce your children to new words. Children will begin to recognize the words if exposed to them multiple times.

Sing a Song

1. Pick a popular toddler song such as "Old MacDonald."

2. Sing this song during diaper changes, at night before bed, in the car, or anytime you like.

Talk

1. Instead of singing, recite the song while feeding your baby or during play time.

2. Talk about the animals in this song.

3. Talk about the sounds these animals make and the letters in their names.

Dancing

1. When "Old MacDonald" comes on Toddler Radio, dance to it.

2. You may also buy this song on various digital radio services.

Sign Language

1. Learn the signs for each animal in "Old MacDonald."

2. While singing or reciting this song, show your child the signs for each animal.

Read

1. Read a book that is based on the "Old MacDonald" song such as *Old MacDonald Had a Farm: Sing Along with Me Board Book* by Nosy Crow/Yu-hsuan Huang.

2. Present the book to your child differently each time you read it. You can do the following:

   - Read it.
   - Sing it.
   - Role-play it (acting like the animals in the book).

Your child will learn and experience the words in the "Old MacDonald" song in various ways. This will help them connect meaning to the words and learn new vocabulary.

CHAPTER 3

Familiarity with Language

FAMILIARITY WITH LANGUAGE

Boys Talk Later than Girls?

Before I had children, child development professionals, friends, and families told me boys usually talk later than girls. It became something that I expected. So, when my son was born, my goal was to communicate with him often so he would become familiar with language.

I didn't want my son to be a late communicator, because in my work as a play therapist, I noticed children who couldn't speak would resort to hitting or kicking out of frustration. However, once they developed language, this behavior would decrease because they could communicate their needs.

My son was able to speak in full sentences by nineteen months. This was because he was naturally exposed to language through play and interaction. I will explain how this was done.

Reading Books Repeatedly

Brown Bear, Brown Bear, What Do You See? was my son's favorite book during his first year of life. He wanted my husband and me to read it over and over again. One time my husband read this book ten times in a row.

Once he learned this story, he was able to anticipate what came next. It made him feel accomplished.

Sometimes, I was somewhat tired of reading the same books repeatedly. However, I was happy that he wanted to read. Below are some tools I used to keep the books interesting.

- Tell the story with missing phrases or blanks. Let the child fill in the blanks.
- Ask the child to identify colors and objects in the pictures.
- Use body language and different voices for the story characters.
- Change your clothes, wear a hat, or say silly phrases while reading.
- Read the story as if you are an animal, like a frog or lion.

Keeping Books Around the House

I wanted to create a literacy-rich home and let my son see words often. Books were kept on all three floors of our home. In the basement, books were in a bin next to Cory's toys. When he wasn't playing with his toys, he would get a book. On the second floor, books were placed as centerpieces on the kitchen table. If he finished with dinner early, then he often grabbed a book while waiting for everyone else to finish. On the third floor, Cory had a book bin in his room. It became a part of his routine to grab books from the bin before naptime and bedtime.

Witnessing Us Read

You've heard the saying, "Kids do what you do and not what you say." I think this is very true. I checked out books from the library for myself and Cory simultaneously. While Cory played independently, I would read my books. He often came up to me while I read and tapped on the book before he could talk. After he could talk, he would look at the words in a book and say "What is that?" Sometimes I would oblige his curiosity and read it to him if appropriate.

Using my fingers to read was one way I showed Cory that the words had meaning. Now when he reads, he uses his finger to read as well.

Finger Play

Using finger play, which is combining hand movement with singing or spoken-words, during songs and talking is a great way to show your child that words have meaning. Let's use the toddler song "Where is Thumbkin?", to the tune of Are You Sleeping? (Frère Jacques), as an example.

Some of the lyrics to this song are as follows:

Where is Thumbkin? Where is Thumbkin?
Here I am! Here I am!
How are you today, sir?
Very well, I thank you

Run away

Run away

When the words, "Here I am," were sung, I showed my son one of my thumbs for Thumbkin. This shows children that, "Here I am," means something is appearing. Additionally, when I sing, "Run away," I take my thumb away. This shows children that "run away" means something is disappearing or going away.

Songs Connected to Books

My son and I listened to Toddler Radio on Pandora often. We listened to this station during playtime and diaper changes. I also purchased CDs with children songs to listen to in the car. I wanted my son to see the words he heard in those songs. Therefore, I checked out books at the library that were based on toddler songs.

When the songs played on Toddler Radio, we quickly grabbed the book to sing and read the lyrics. Before bedtime, I would sing the song while following along in the book. This activity allowed Cory to hear the words and see them. It was preparing him to read and spell.

Play

Cory learned a lot of language through play. Using descriptive language during playtime assists in connecting actions with words. It also exposes kids to new vocabulary. If we played with a ball, I would roll it to him on the floor and say, "Look at the tiny blue ball rolling fast toward you." This is teaching him size, colors, and the concept of speed.

I taught Cory action verbs through playing with balls as well. When he bounced the ball against the wall, I stated, "Look at the green ball ricochet against the wall." If he did it again, I would make the observation that the green ball is bouncing against the wall and coming back to him.

Library

Cory and I took our very first trip to the library together when I was three months pregnant with him. I checked out about ten books at a time and read them to my belly at night. When Cory was two months old, we went to our first Baby and Me library program.

The Baby and Me program (may be called something else if your area library provides one) involves a librarian reading books and singing songs to babies, sometimes while being held by their moms or playing on the floor. They also have toys that babies can play with, like balls, rattles, and soft stuffed animals. This provided more exposure to language but from a different perspective.

The librarian read various books and sometimes would sing songs in a tone and tune different than I would at home. Some songs would involve the babies doing actions such as clapping and being lifted in the air by parents. This provided connections of actions and words for Cory.

We also played outside of the Baby and Me Program at the library. Our library has toys, puzzles, and manipulative wall toys that kids can play with. This is a great way to get your child in the environment of books. There are times when we don't read in the library, and instead Cory will spend his time playing with toys. Before leaving the library, we usually choose several books to borrow.

TIP: Our library allows us to borrow fifty books per library card. Get plenty of books so you can space out your trips to the library. Don't forget to renew and/or return the books on time. If not, you will have a late fee.

Acting Out Books

Combining reading and physical activity is a great way to expose children to new vocabulary. In the morning, Cory would sit in the high chair while I was preparing breakfast. During this time, I would act out books. Of course, I had to role play *Brown Bear, Brown Bear, What Do You See?*, which you know was his favorite book at the time.

I read it so much, I started to memorize it. Reciting the book, along with other books, while acting out the animals in the story, became a part of our morning routine. For the bear, I would curl my fingers and make growling noises. For the duck, I would flap my bent arms and say "Quack, Quack." This eventually led to Cory opening this book and doing the motions for animals. This was done before he started speaking.

Books or Songs with Instructions

One of my favorite children's songs is *Run Baby Run* by Raffi. Part of the lyrics to this song are as follows:

Run baby run

Run run run run run

Jump baby jump

Jump jump jump jump jump

Spin baby spin

Round and round and round

Sing baby sing

La la la la la

Clap baby clap

Clap clap clap clap clap

Dance baby dance

Dance dance dance dance dance

And then you swing baby swing

Swing swing swing swing swing

And then you run baby run

Run run run run run

This song has a catchy beat and action verbs. We often played this song on YouTube and did the movements. It taught my son how to spin, run, jump, etc. YouTube has a video where the lyrics come on the screen. You guessed it: he was learning how to spell and recognize those action verbs during this song.

This is me taking a selfie with Cory in the middle of doing finger play. I loved to sit with him in the play gate and do various movements to songs. He was waiting for the next song and not paying attention to the camera.

ACTIVITIES

Try to incorporate the activities below at least once a week with your children to get them familiar with language.

Finger Play

1. Use the five songs below to do finger play with your child.
2. If they are able to, have them do the finger play along with you.
3. Make it fun by putting on a hat or dressing in a costume.

The songs are as follows:

- "Itsy Bitsy Spider"
- "Five Little Monkeys"
- "Wheels on the Bus"
- "Rock, Scissors, Paper"
- "Open Shut Them"

Songs Connected to Books

1. Purchase or borrow the books below from your local library.
2. Find the songs on Pandora Toddler Radio Station or YouTube.
3. Use the books to read the lyrics along with the song.

4. Point out the lyrics as you are singing.

   - *Sing and Sing Along: Itsy Bitsy Spider by Annie Kubler*
   - *The Wheels on the Bus by Raffi*
   - *Baby Beluga (Songs to Read) by Raffi*
   - *Old MacDonald Had a Farm: Sing Along with Me by Nosy Crow and Yu-hsuan Huang*
   - *The Bear Went Over the Mountain (Sing-Along Songs) by Steven Anderson and Tim Palin*

Library

1. While you are at the library borrowing books, ask the librarians about their programs for babies, toddlers, and kids in general.

2. Sign up for those programs either online or while you are at the library.

3. Remember to sign up quickly for the programs, because they tend to fill up fast.

Play

1. During play with your child, remember to use descriptive words to tell what is happening.

2. Be sure to add in new words while you play, as well as repeat words your child is already familiar with.

Acting Out Books

1. Purchase or borrow audiobooks from your library.

2. Play the audiobooks at home and in the car.

3. While the narrator is reading the book, act out the story with your child.

4. You may also act out books you have read with your child.

Songs with Instructions

1. Play the songs below through YouTube or Toddler Radio at home.

2. Dance and follow the instructions to these songs with your child.

3. Sing the lyrics while dancing so your child can make connections between the words and movements.

- "Head, Shoulders, Knees, and Toes"
- "The Hokey Pokey"
- "Father Abraham"
- "The Dinosaur Stomp"
- "The Wheels on the Bus"
- "Teddy Bear, Teddy Bear"

CHAPTER 4

In-Depth Learning

IN-DEPTH LEARNING

What Is In-Depth Learning?

In-depth learning is being exposed to a concept in various ways. I used the five senses and various learning styles to expose my son to the alphabet, new words, and reading. As you know, the five senses are hearing, seeing, touching, tasting, and smelling. Let's use the example of a parent wanting to teach their child words in the food category. A parent may do the following:

- View a food magazine with the child. **(sight)**
- Draw pictures of food on a menu and label it. **(sight)**
- Read a children's book aloud about food to and with the child. **(sight and hearing)**
- Listen to an audiobook about food in the car. **(hearing)**
- Create a song with the child about fruits and vegetables. **(hearing)**
- Play grocery store with play food and a cash register. **(physical/rhythmic/kinesthetic)**
- Do a scavenger hunt with play food or pictures of food from a magazine. **(physical/rhythmic/kinesthetic)**

How to Make In-Depth Learning Fun

- Do not hold long sessions with young children when trying to expose them to the reading. (Fifteen to twenty minutes of daily reading is great.)
- If the child wants to read more than twenty minutes, then follow their lead.
- Tailor the lessons to their interests.
- Expose the child to words and reading in various ways through play, reading, toys, interaction with you, digital media, etc.
- Learn what your child's definition of fun is and incorporate this into learning.
- Play games—games incorporate all learning styles.

Learning Styles

Learning styles is an important part of making learning fun and relaxing to children. You will learn how children with specific learning styles communicate and their favorite toys and activities to do.

Auditory Learners

Children who use **hearing** to learn are usually **auditory** learners. Below are communication methods, activities, and toys to help these children learn new words and how to read in a fun way.

Communication

- Tend to remember concepts when explained aloud
- Like to repeat aloud what they have learned
- Can retain knowledge when paired with music or clapping

Toy or Activities

- Like music
- Can remember words to songs
- Good at following spoken directions
- Like being read to
- Like wordplay and language patterns

Visual Learners

Children who use **sight** to learn are usually **visual** learners. Below are specific communication methods, activities, and toys to help your child learn new words and how to read in a fun way.

Communication

- Communicate through drawing and painting
- Like reading and retelling stories
- Will say, "Show me," when learning something new

Toys or Activities

- Books

- Drawing or viewing pictures
- Puzzles
- Creating storylines with sketches
- Colorful Flashcards

Kinesthetic/Physical (Rhythm) Learners

Children who use **touch** to learn are usually **kinesthetic** learners. Below are methods, activities, and toys to help these children learn new words and how to read in a fun way.

Communication

- Learn through touch and movement
- Like to say, "Let me see that," which means, "Let me hold that."
- Like to use action words such as run, jump, play, kick

Toys or Activities

- Like building and model sets
- Enjoy interactive displays at museums
- Love to tear things apart to learn

Many young children possess more than one learning style. We will discuss later how to work with children with more than one learning style. You can incorporate communication tactics and activities from all learning styles and see which one your child gravitates toward.

If you see your child struggling to grasp certain words, expose them to those words in a way that coincides with how they learn best.

Cory is independently putting together a jigsaw puzzle made up of three-letter and four-letter words. This puzzle incorporates the three learning styles because he is assembling the puzzle (kinesthetic), saying the words (auditory), and looking at colorful images (visual).

ACTIVITIES

Below are reading games/activities for specific learning styles.

Visual Learner Reading Activities

1. Draw and paint colorful pictures with your child and label them.

2. When learning words, "show them the word" through

    - books,
    - magazines,
    - real-world items,
    - and digital media.

3. Get books with colorful pictures and point to each word when reading.

4. Get puzzles with pictures and words.

5. Create stories with characters and dialogue.

6. Use colorful flashcards with words.

7. Use colorful word charts or boards with words (for examples, boards with the family schedule or food menu).

8. Have the child draw their interpretation of a book.

9. Use window markers to create a story or to draw and write words in a certain category.

10. Build letters that form words with blocks and a magnetic tiles playset.

11. Watch educational television reading shows such as *Super Y* and the LeapFrog series.

12. Identify words while in the world or while you are running errands:

    - Read directions.
    - Read signs.
    - Read advertisements.
    - Go to museums and read new information.

13. Play a word hunt game:

    - Hide words in a certain category around your home and have children find and identify the words.

Auditory Learners Reading Activities

1. Read books that are based on songs:

    - Make it fun by playing instruments while singing.
    - Some books based on songs are as follows:
    - *What a Wonderful World* by Bob Thiele/George David Weiss and sung by Louis Armstrong
    - *Take Us Out to the Ball Game* (Sesame Street) by Constance Allen/Tom Brannon
    - *Every Little Thing* by Bob Marley/Vanessa Brantley-Newton
    - *Singing in the Rain* by Arthur Freed/Nacio Herb Brown
    - *Coat of Many Colors* by Dolly Parton

2. Listen to audiobooks in the car or at home and read along with the narrator. These can be borrowed from the library and purchased online or at your local bookstore.

3. Write words in a certain category outside with sidewalk chalk and then give the child directions to run or hop to certain words you call out.

4. Make up a silly song or chant together.

5. Make up bedtime stories.

6. Read various books aloud, which may include the following:

    - Comic books
    - Autobiography or biography

- How-to books
- Fact books – which give expertise on a certain subject being shared
- Geography or travel books

7. Record a video of the child or the parent reading and identifying objects in the book. Play the video back so the child can hear it.

8. Play word games:
   - Little Treasures Matching Letter Game
   - Melissa & Doug See & Spell Learning Toy

9. Play bingo games where words must be identified.

10. Spell words with magnetic letters.

11. Play a word hunt game (auditory style): hide words in a certain category around your home and have children read directions (you have written) aloud to find and identify the words.

12. Retell books you have just read, but change the ending.

13. Play Find-A-Rhyme: Write down a word, and then have the child tell you rhyming words associated with the written word. For example, if you write the word man, the child may respond by saying, "Can, fan, tan . . ." A variation of this game is to give the child a certain amount of time (like fifteen seconds) to say the rhyming words.

Kinesthetic Learner Reading Activities

1. Hold and manipulate refrigerator letters to make words.
2. Use the letters from wooden alphabet blocks to make words.
3. Do sand play with materials such as sand, measuring cups, spoons, shovels, and funnels.
   - Place labels on materials used for play.
   - Use descriptive words during play, such as *mix*, *mold*, *dig*, *pour*, *big*, and *bigger*.
4. Go outside and collect objects in nature, such as rocks, leaves, flowers, pinecones, seeds, dirt.
   - Write categories of items on cards, such as rocks, plants, and leaves, and sort them.
   - Talk about the difference in the objects and write down those words.
5. Make various characters using Play-Doh, and then create a story with those characters.
6. Let your child make a snack by listening to instructions. The next day, let your child make the same snack with written instructions.
7. Let your child give you movement or action verbs, such as *jump*, *skip*, *gallop*, and *crawl*.
   a. Write down the words your child says on cards.
   b. Tell your child to do the actions on the cards as you hold them up.

    c. At first you may have to read the words. Eventually they will be able to read the words on the cards independently.

8. Have children sit on a bouncy ball, and verbally give them instructions on various directions to move:

    a. For example, you may say, "Hop forward five times."

    b. Next time do the same activity with written words and verbally: say and write, "Hop forward five times."

    c. Next time, do not speak, just write, "Hop forward five times," and let them read it.

9. Dance, clap, and snap while chanting a story with rhythm and rhymes, such as *Chicka Chicka Boom Boom* by Bill Martin or *Who Took the Cookie from the Cookie Jar* by Bonnie Lass and Philemon Sturges.

10. Write a popular children's song on a big piece of paper, such as "Twinkle, Twinkle, Little Star"

    a. Have the child find a certain word, like *star*, in the song.

    b. Give the child a crayon to put an X on the word

    c. Keep doing this activity with different words in the song.

11. Take your child outside to play and tell them to pay attention to what they see.

    a. Have your child describe to you what they saw, and then you draw what they are describing.

b. After drawing, label each object with your child.

12. Read interactive pop-up books such as the following:
    - *Alpha Bugs: A Pop-up Alphabet* by David Carter
    - *The Wide-Mouthed Frog* by Keith Faulkner
    - *Lego: Pop-Up* by Matthew Reinhart
    - *Disney Princess: A Magical Pop-Up World* by Matthew Reinhart

CHAPTER 5

Learning the Alphabet

EVERYDAY NATURAL EXPOSURE

Cory learned the alphabet at eighteen months. "A" was one of his first few words after "dada" and "ball." I thought he would learn the alphabet at three or four years old. So this discovery blew my mind. He was exposed to the letters through play, fun interaction, and doing our everyday routine. I never used worksheets or flashcards.

Below I will explain how he was naturally exposed to the alphabet.

In His Room

Before my son was born, my husband and I decided his room theme would be ABC 123. While pregnant, I was listening to a lot of Jackson 5 music, and their hit song, "ABC" was my favorite. We purchased alphabet stickers with pictures for each letter as borders around his room. We put colorful pictures in his room so he could have something appealing to view while lying down.

I remember reading an alphabet book to Cory before bedtime, and he looked up and pointed to the alphabet and then back at the book. He made the connection that the alphabet was in his room. From that day on, he would continue to look up and admire the letters.

Singing

When my son woke in the middle of the night as a baby, I had to find a way to soothe him and myself. I was so tired! Singing and rocking in the chair was a way to calm Cory down. The alphabet song was familiar, and I could sing it while half sleeping with one eye closed. I coupled this with rubbing and patting his back. While singing, my son's brain was absorbing the rhythm and words that would later lead him to reading. He also associated the song with pleasure and comfort.

Play

My son's daycare provider sent a video of Cory playing with alphabet blocks. When he saw the *A* block, he said "A." Once I saw this, we began to play with the alphabet. The purpose of this was to connect what he was familiar with, the alphabet, with fun and games. We constructed letters with his Duplo Lego blocks, which are the large blocks for babies and toddlers. We also made letters with Play-Doh and Magnetic Tiles.

When we went outside to play, I would identify letters on car license plates and signs. This was done before he could speak in full sentences.

Music

One of our favorite activities to do was listen to Toddler Radio while playing. On Pandora Toddler Radio we heard the alphabet song in various tunes and rhythms. My favorite version was by Basho Mosko because it had a great beat. Whenever we heard that song, I would pick Cory up and dance with him. He became so quiet and calm during these moments.

During a car ride is a great time to play music. I purchased a CD by Mark D. Pencil called *Learning with Hip Hop*. I played this CD in the car because I was tired of singing to Cory in the car. Our car stereo was broken at the time, and when he cried I would sing toddler songs. Once our radio was repaired, I played this CD, which has a hip-hop version of the alphabet.

I found a YouTube video version of the Mark D. Pencil alphabet song. After lunch or dinner, we often turned the video on and danced to it.

Books

My son loved when I read alphabet books to him because they had colorful and fun images. They also presented the letters to him in a variety of ways. We have read over fifty various types of alphabet books. This was exposure to over fifty ways of looking at the letters, countless vocabulary words, pictures, and stories.

We made reading fun by acting out the books. For example, if *H* was for *hop*, we would hop around the house. If *S* was for *snake*, we would crawl around the house like a snake. This made the alphabet come alive!

Writing

During long car rides with my son, I would sit in the back seat with him. When he was awake, I would draw silly pictures and write letters. Before he could talk he pointed to the paper, which was code for write another letter. We also did this during long church services (to keep him quiet) and in waiting rooms.

Once my son could talk, he would say the letter and then I would write it. This activity empowered him because he was able to put his communication skills to use.

Other fun activities were writing the alphabet and pictures connected with the letters in the bathtub, outside with chalk, and on the window with window markers. For example, after writing *A*, I then would draw an apple or an ape.

Digital Media

Technology can be a great supplement to your child's learning. After my son was eighteen months and learned the ABC's, I allowed him to watch the show *Leapfrog: Phonics Farm*. By this time, he could understand what was going on in this cartoon. This particular video reviews the alphabet and phonics with a catchy storyline, characters, and songs. The video provides a visual in which my son saw the letters of the alphabet moving and talking to one another. The characters in the cartoon showed my son how the letters come together to make words. It gave him a deeper meaning of why the alphabet is so important to communication and language.

We also watched videos such as the following (content in parenthesis is where the video can be found):

- Leapfrog Letter Factory video (Amazon)
- Leapfrog Phonics Farm video (Amazon)
- "ABC Songs for Children" by Cocomelon Nursery Rhymes (YouTube)
- "Do You Know Your Alphabet Song?" by Mark D. Pencil (YouTube)
- Sesame Street television show (PBS Kids, HBO Kids, WETA Kids)
- Bob the Train ABC Songs (YouTube)
- "Learn the Alphabet with Blippi" (YouTube)
- Super Why (The cartoon has the "ABC Song" in each episode. It is an advanced show because it involves reading words) (PBS Kids)
- "Mother Goose Club ABC Song" (YouTube)
- "Alphabet Songs" by Have Fun Teaching (YouTube)

Sign Language

While traveling by car and during breakfast and dinner time, I would sign the alphabet to my son. It was used as a visual aid and was another way to expose him to the alphabet. He was amazed that my fingers would move along with the song. He soon realized that letters could be communicated by using your hands.

Cory made the letter P with gears and widgets.

ACTIVITIES FOR ALPHABET RECOGNITION

Alphabet Free Course

I recommend you take our free course: How to Teach the Alphabet in a Fun Way.

For more information please visit SimplyOutrageousYouth.org

Hands-On Alphabet Activities

1. Create a colorful chart using crayons, paint, and stickers of the alphabet. Display this artwork in your home.
2. Use window markers to draw the alphabet.
3. Use Mega Bloks, Legos, and Magnetic Tiles to build alphabet letters.
4. Identify the alphabet on errands or during outside play in the following places:
    - License plates
    - Signs and billboards
    - Advertisement in stores
5. Write letters in the sand or mud.

6. Play the alphabet hunt game: hide letters around a room and have children find and identify them.
7. Sing the "ABC Song." Make it fun by playing instruments (bought or homemade) while singing.
8. Make up a silly song or chant together about the alphabet.
9. Give your child magnetic refrigerator letters to hold and manipulate.
10. Have your child sit on a bouncy ball while singing and chanting the alphabet.
11. Dance, clap, and snap while reading or practicing the alphabet.
12. Dance to catchy alphabet songs on YouTube, Pandora Toddler Radio, an MP3 player, or CDs.
13. Use alphabet stamps to make artwork.
14. Use Legos and Magnetic Tiles to build the alphabet.
15. Read alphabet pop-up books or books with rhythm and rhyme:
    - Alpha Bugs: A Pop-Up Alphabet by David Carter
    - *A is for Animals* by David Pelham
    - Chicka Boom Boom by Bill Martin
16. Dip the bottom of toy cars in paint and have children trace letters on a big sheet of paper.
17. Have children play with bathtub foam letters.

CHAPTER 6

Phonics

PHONICS

This is a short chapter because I did not spend a lot of time on phonics. My son learned to make the letter sounds while learning alphabet recognition. He was exposed to the phonics through natural learning and reading.

Singing and Music

I mentioned previously that singing was how I soothed my son and myself when he woke up in the middle of the night as a baby. One of my favorite songs to sing was the "ABC Song." While singing the letters, I also incorporated the phonics. I made up the song as I went along. I would sing the following lyrics:

A is for Apple AAA Apple, and A is for Ape AAA Ape

B is Balloon BBB Balloon.

This song incorporated the letter sounds as well as the long and short vowel sounds. During the day, we sung this song with an upbeat rhythm. Many times, we used our do-it-yourself instruments, like a water bottle shaker with rice or our oatmeal container drum for music and added fun.

On YouTube, there are a lot of phonic songs that my son liked. After dinner, we viewed these videos and danced to them.

Toys and Art

A family member gave Cory an alphabet train puzzle from Learning Resources that he loved putting together. When we put this puzzle together, I identified the sounds and words associated with the letter. For example, for letter *A*, I said, "*A* is for Alligator, AA Alligator." My son waited until I identified the sound of the letter before putting the next piece on the puzzle. I also repeated these steps whenever we played or made artwork with the alphabet.

One toy I highly recommend is LeapFrog's Tad's Fridge Phonics Magnets. It teaches kids letter sounds through songs. Kids can also manipulate the letters and make words.

Books

Books played a big role in teaching my son phonics. We read a variety of alphabet books, which meant he saw many words that begin with each letter. I would make the sound for each letter as we read. I incorporated all sounds for letters; for example, *C* has two sounds, the hard sound in *cut* and the soft sound in *celery*.

Television

Cory's favorite cartoon was *Phonics Farm* by Leapfrog. This twenty-minute cartoon is about Scout and his friends traveling to a magical farm to see a collection of letter animals. They learn phonics and the alphabet and make new friends along the way. This cartoon also addresses the vowels and the long sounds they make.

Another great show is *Alphablocks*. This shows addresses letter phonics and other sounds such as ar, oo, ee, th, ch, and many more. This can be found on YouTube and Amazon.

Cory playing with the LeapFrog Tad's Fridge Phonic Magnets letters.

ACTIVITIES

Below are activities that will make learning phonics fun!

What Sound Is It?

1. Get items from around the house, such as an apple, a cup, a ball, and a block.

2. Help your child identify the items' first letter sound by putting a magnetic letter or written letter on separate pieces of paper beneath it. For example, if you have an apple, emphasize the "aaa" sound and have the child place an *A* beneath it.

3. Once your child becomes familiar with the sound, offer less help until they can identify the first letter sound in the word independently.

Magic with Rhyming

1. Use magnetic letters or written letters on separate pieces of paper to form the word *bat*.

2. Now change the word to *cat* by replacing the *b* with a *c*.

3. Then spell other words such as *sat*, *mat*, *hat*, and *rat*.

Find a Sound

1. Pick a letter and identify its sounds.

2. Take turns going around your home or outside finding items that start with that sound.

3. For example, if you pick the letter *A*, go outside and find an acorn.

Jump On It

1. Go outside and write the alphabet with sidewalk chalk.

2. Make a letter sound.

3. Have your child jump on the letter associated with the sound you just made.

4. Make it fun by racing, where you and your child compete to jump on the letter first.

CHAPTER 7

Blending Sounds

BLENDING SOUNDS

Magnetic Letters and Other Toys

Once my son learned the phonics, we started using magnetic letters to blend sounds. I first tried this when my son was twenty-one months. I put together the word *cat* using the letters and sounded it out. Then I put together the words, *pig*, *man*, and *hug* and sounded them out. Next, I put together the word *pot* and asked him to give me the letter it began with. I first sounded out "p," and my son gave me the letter *p*. Then I sounded the short *o*, and he gave me *o*. Last, I sounded out "t", and he gave me the letter *t*. I repeated this with various three-letter words for the next five minutes, and he understood the concept.

The next day, he asked to make words on the refrigerator again. This time, I asked him if he could spell the word /k/-/i/-/d/ and he independently used the letters to spell the words. We repeated these steps with other three-letter words as this became a game to him.

We did this same activity with toys that we used to build letters, such as Magnetic Tiles, Play-Doh, and blocks. We built the letters first and then made words by blending the sounds together.

Writing

One of our favorite activities is to write stories. We usually get a big sheet of craft paper and create stories about my son's favorite animal, toy, or friend. Sometimes, we will use a story that we previously read and change the ending. We divide the paper in half and write the story on top and draw or paint pictures on the bottom.

My son will write one word, and then I will write another word. When he is unable to spell a word, he will sound it out first. If necessary, he will seek my assistance. I occasionally pretend that can't spell a word and ask for his assistance in sounding it out. This boosts his confidence because he has the skills to figure out how to spell words and to help me as well.

Reading

In my experience, the best way to learn how to spell and blend sounds is through reading. There are so many phonic rules and exceptions in the English language that a child could learn. Instead of focusing on memorizing them, it is better to engage them in actually reading.

My son has more of a desire to sound out a word if it will give him the plot or meaning of a story. This is especially true if he is interested in what the characters will do next.

When my son started reading, I purposely got books with three-letter and four-letter words. I also got a variety of books for my son so he could see those words repeatedly in different stories. My library permits us to borrow fifty books at a time, and I am always at my limit. Weekly, I will take ten books back and check out another ten. These types of books are short, so we read them quickly.

One strategy I used to promote the use of blending sounds is to take note of the words he had trouble sounding out and then incorporating them into our play. For example, if he had trouble with the word *rope*, I would create a rope with Play-Doh the next time we played with it. Then I may tell a story about a rope while playing, making sure to include the spelling within my story.

Other Connections

I make it a daily practice to play and observe my son to gather information about his interests and curiosities. With this information, I will make connections through play with language. For example, one day we were reading a book about the various foods kids eat all over the world. In this book, the words *food* and *good* appeared frequently.

My son loves the cartoon *Alphablocks*, which had an episode teaching children about the *oo* sound. We watched this episode together, and Cory made the observation that the word *food* had two *O*'s in it. He also became excited when he saw the words *good* and *food*. This episode also showcased words like *hood*, *cool*, *cook*, and *boot*. We took it a step further and started building those words with Legos.

I also would say the *oo* words during the day. I would ask Cory about his *mood* or if the *food* I *cooked* for lunch was *good*. There are various ways to make connections; you just have to be creative.

Cory independently spelled the word dig by blending letter sounds when he was twenty-one months.

ACTIVITIES

Below are activities that will make blending sounds fun!

Build the Word

1. You will need three bowls, two sets of the twenty-six alphabet letters, and one set of vowels (including y).

2. Put one set of the twenty-six alphabet letters into the first bowl.

3. Put one set of vowels in the second bowl.

4. Put the other set of twenty-six alphabet letters into the third bowl.

5. Take turns drawing out letters from each bowl.

6. If you can make a real three-letter word with your cards, then keep them.

7. If you can't, return them.

8. Help each other during your turns.

Create the Environment

1. Have your child create functional signs and notes for your home.

2. Assist your child in writing these notes.

3. Sometimes pretend you can't spell a word and need your child's expertise to help you sound the word out.

4. If your child cannot write, have them draw and you write the words. You are still exposing them to words with this variation.

5. Below are ideas of signs and notes you and your child could write for your home:

   - Grocery list
   - A sign identifying their room; e.g., Cory's room.
   - "Quiet, I am napping," sign
   - Breakfast, lunch, or dinner menu

What Is It?

1. Get items from around the house, such as a pot, cup, ball, and block.

2. Help your child name the item by arranging magnetic letters or written letters on separate pieces of paper beneath it. For example, if you have a pot, emphasize the /p/-/o/-/t/ sound and have the child place the letters *P O T* beneath it.

3. Once your child becomes familiar with the spelling, offer less help until they can spell it independently.

CHAPTER 8

Sight Words

SIGHT WORDS

Sight words are those we identify by their appearance and *not* by sounding them out. Please view examples of sight words at the end of this book. In order to be proficient readers, a child must know numerous sight words. I know many people who use flashcards to teach sight words. I have never felt comfortable showing a baby or toddler flashcards. It is not my style of teaching, and it would make it boring for my child. My son learned sight words through play, books, and digital media.

Recording the Day with Words

Cory and I love to learn on the spot. This means if we see anything intriguing, we will make a fun learning experience out of it. One day, after putting his magnetic letters in alphabetical order, Cory stood up, and I noticed he was getting big and tall. Then I decided to communicate my thoughts by arranging the letters to say, "The boy is big." I read what I wrote and told him that he is a big boy. He got excited and wanted to create more sentences.

We looked around the room and made more sentences like, "I see two balls," and, "We will get the ball and play." This was the beginning of teaching my son sight words. We used them to communicate what we saw.

I also wrote short sentences to tell him to do certain things. For example, one day I arranged the letters to say, "Put the blue cup on the table." Then, with my assistance, he created sentences to answer me, like, "All done." If he was not able to spell a sight word, I helped him spell it and then tried to use that same word in my sentences.

Writing

Cory was able to write the entire alphabet as a two-year-old. When he was twelve months he would watch me write the alphabet on the window with windows markers, on long road trips, and on paper in waiting rooms. We also formed the alphabet with Play-Doh. The combination of these activities assisted in him learning how each letter was formed. When he had the strength to pick up crayons or markers, he made an A because it was inputted in his brain. He wrote his first A at 21 months.

I used fun ways to practice his writing, which in turn helped him to learn sight words. He wrote birthday and thank-you cards to family members. I usually would write on a separate paper the words "Happy Birthday to . . ." (and put a family's member's name there).

Our favorite activity was to go outside and write short sentences about what we saw. If we saw a dog walking, we would write a sentence about that. For example, one sentence said, "The black dog is walking with the woman."

Also, he would draw pictures. His day care provider had him practicing basic lines and curves along with the other kids. This helped to hone his writing skills.

Books

Whenever I read books to Cory, I would use my finger to follow along so he would understand that the text had meaning. Sometimes after reading a sentence, I would point out sight words such as *the*, *that*, *those*, or *because*. It was a reminder that we used the same words in a sentence we wrote previously.

The more books a child reads, the more they are exposed to sight words. We always have at least fifty library books in our home. Then we have some books that I have purchased. Children viewing sight words while reading can see how they connect to make a complete thought. I think flash cards is an isolated way of teaching because the child is just seeing the words and not how they fit into a sentence. However, putting a bunch of segregated words on flash cards and connecting them to make sentences is effective.

This is not to say flash cards do not work for many kids. I am just stating my opinion here on how to make it more fun and engaging for the child, and something they are willing to participate in.

YouTube

As soon as my son started to notice sight words in books, I would let him view them in songs on YouTube. The YouTube sight word songs were appealing to Cory and I because they contained a catchy beat with lots of bright colors. It made sight words fun! Sometimes, we would put the video on just to dance to it. Then when we created sentences or read books, Cory became excited because he saw those words in the YouTube video.

We watched a variety of these types of videos, so my son learned numerous words.

Nursery Rhymes

Reading, repeating, listening, and watching nursery rhymes is an excellent way to expose children to sight words. Some of my son's favorite nursery rhymes were "Baa Baa Black Sheep," "Bingo Was His Name-O," "Eeny, Meeny, Miny, Moe," and "Humpty Dumpty." I will show you how I used nursery rhymes to expose Cory to sight words. Let's use "Humpty Dumpty" as an example.

"Humpty Dumpty" has sight words such as *had*, *great*, *the*, *a*, *couldn't*, *put*, *together*, and *again*. Cory first heard this nursery rhyme in a free Mommy and Me swimming class we took when he was four months old. Then I borrowed nursery rhyme books from the library so we could see, hear, and read the lyrics. On YouTube, Mother Goose Company featured a sing-along cartoon with captions. This was beneficial because Cory could see the words to the song on the television. It also provided us with opportunities to move because we could dance to the song. However, sometimes he would be fascinated with seeing the words on the screen and he would stop dancing to look at the words.

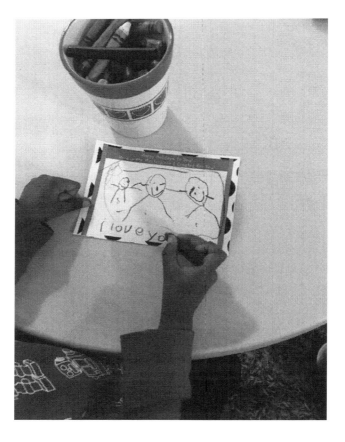

Cory writing the sight words I love you to a family member on a holiday card.

ACTIVITIES

Below are activities that will make learning sight words fun!

Give Me the Word

1. Write five sight words on separate pieces of paper, such as *is*, *the*, *these*, *that*, and *over*. Increase the number you write as your child learns more sight words

2. Place your child's stuffed animals, puppets, and toys on a chair, couch, or table.

3. Read one of the sight words on the paper aloud.

4. Instruct your child to give one of the words to a particular toy. For example, you may state "Elephant wants to eat the word 'is.'"

5. Then use the sight word in a sentence: "Elephant is hungry."

6. Repeat this same step until all the words are given to all the animals.

7. Assist your child in the beginning.

8. As they learn the words, gradually have them play this game independently.

Get Them Off!

1. Write five sight words on Post-It notepaper. Increase this number as your child learns more sight words

2. Stick these words to different parts on your body, like your forehead, nose, arm, hand, legs, and foot.

3. Call out one of the sight words and then have your child take the word and put it in a bowl.

4. Then use the sight word in a sentence.

5. Assist your child by pointing to the words as you say them, if they are beginners

6. Repeat this until you have no words on your body.

7. As they learn the words, gradually have them play this game with more words and more independently.

Create a Book

1. Write five sight words on paper. Increase this number as your child learns more sight words

2. Create a short and simple book with your child, including the sight words. A book may consist of a few sheets of paper stapled at the edge.

3. Have the child create the main character(s). The characters could be the child's favorite toy or friend.

4. Create a short book where there is one sentence on each page.

5. Remember to draw pictures for the story.

The Matching Game

1. Write five sight words on paper. Increase this number as your child learns more sight words.

2. Create two copies of each sight word on index cards.

3. Spread the cards on a table or floor.

4. Take turns playing the matching game.

    a. First the child will turn over one card. Then he will try to turn over another card with that same word on it. If your child turns over the word "that," for example, he must turn over another card.

    b. If he finds "that" on the second card, then he can keep both cards.

    c. If he does not find the other "that" card, then he must turn both cards over again.

    d. Once a match is found, create a sentence with the sight word.

    e. Then it is your turn.

5. Assist your child at first when it is their turn.

6. As they learn the words, gradually have them play their turn independently.

CHAPTER 9

Experience

EXPERIENCE

Utilizing real-world experiences is one of the best ways to teach kids to read. It allows a child to see the words come alive. It provides hands-on activities that a kinesthetic learner needs, the sounds that authority learners love, and the rich images that visual learners like to view. I will give five examples of how various experiences encouraged and taught my son to read.

Zoos

When Cory was a baby I began teaching him animal sounds. My son likes the book *Good Night, Gorilla* by Peggy Rathmann. This book mentions numerous animals, such as a gorilla, elephant, giraffe, lion, hyena, and armadillo. I took this book to the zoo with us, and it was an enriching experience. Cory was fifteen months at the time. When we saw the lions, I pulled out the book and showed my son where they were in the book. I also pointed to each letter in the lion's name and compared that to the sign at the zoo. He kept looking back and forth from the book to the lions in amazement.

When we got to the elephant, I identified it in the book as well. Then when we saw the giraffe he said "book." I had forgotten a giraffe was in the book. I started turning the pages in the book and found the giraffe. I was amazed that he caught on to our activity and reminded me giraffes were in the book.

Farm

Cory and I have read a lot of books about farm animals. Therefore, I was so excited to take him to a petting zoo, where he could pet and feed the animals. He was seventeen months when we first visited, and this time he wanted to hold the book, *The Petting Zoo* by DK Publishing. When we saw a farm animal, I would identify the sign with the animal's name. Our routine was for him to identify the animals in the book, feed them, sanitize his hands, and then get the book to identify the next animal.

This gave him the opportunity to hear the animals sounds I often made for each animal, while reading in real time. He also was able to touch them, see how they live on the farm, and see what they eat.

Museum

One of the first museums my son experienced was the Science Center. At daycare, his teacher showed the children a video about space, and somehow, at twenty months, he was able to get the same video on my smartphone using YouTube. My daycare provider said she noticed him paying attention to the letters she typed to get to the "Space Song."

Once I saw he was interested in space, I got some books from the library about the solar system. We read the books repeatedly until he knew the eight planets and five dwarf planets. He was also able to recite some facts about each planet. The next step was to take him to a science museum and visit the planetarium.

When we arrived at the museum we found out he could wear an astronaut uniform for a short period of time during the day. Again, I took our solar system book and we identified the planets and the spelling of their names. We played a game where he had to put the planets in order. Because we read the solar system book continuously, he knew this like the back of his hand. The game included many facts he knew already about the planets. We compared what was written in the game to the book. There was also a machine that allowed him to rotate the planets around the sun. He told us he had so much fun.

Also, my husband put the solar system in his room so he will never forget the planets. This is reading comprehension at its best.

Role Playing

A great activity for reading comprehension is role playing. Role playing really allows your child to absorb books through reading, hearing, seeing, and playing.

I incorporate role playing into our reading time in many ways. One way is to play audiobooks in our home and act them out as the narrator reads the book. We have done this with the book *The Three Little Pigs*. Cory would play each pig, and then my husband or I would play the wolf. In the book, three pigs are making houses out of different materials, while the wolf's mission is to blow their houses down and eat them. My son pretends like he is building the houses and is afraid of the wolf.

Another way to role-play a book is by performing the actions while reading. For example, if we are reading about a character that is running, we will get up in the middle of the book and run. We recently read the book called *Animalphabet* by Julia Donaldson. In this book, each letter represents an animal. After reading about a letter and its animal association, we role-played that animal around the house. It was a fun activity! Cory wanted to keep reading and role-playing that book repeatedly.

Games and Hands-On Activities

Games and hands-on activities are a great way to teach kids new vocabulary, increase listening skills, and boost reading comprehension. They incorporate various learning styles, such as auditory, visual, and kinesthetic learning. On the next page, I have given you five games we used to help my son learn to read.

ACTIVITIES

Change the Story

Children should be provided opportunities to apply knowledge from books through imaginative play. Below is a way to stimulate your child's ability to problem solve, sort information, and develop new ideas through creative-thinking questions. Below is how to do it:

1. Read a story to your child.

2. Ensure your child is familiar with the story. You may have to read the story multiple times to your child.

3. Have your child change the ending.

4. They may communicate their version of the ending through the following:

    a. Drawing a picture

    b. Creating a sculpture with Play-Doh or clay

    c. Creating a dance

    d. Role-playing with props

    e. Simply telling the story

Clues from the Story

The following activity will develop your child's listening skills. It is also great for reading comprehension and learning new vocabulary.

1. Read a story to your child.

2. Ensure your child is familiar with the story. You may have to read the story multiple times to your child.

3. Gather clues from the story you have read. Clues from the story can include the following:

    a. Characters

    b. Setting—where the story took place

    c. The conflict or problem in the story

    d. The story's resolution

    e. Basically anything in the story

4. Let your child guess what you are thinking of from the story with the clues you give them.

5. Use descriptive words to describe your clue, such as, "I'm thinking of a humongous animal with a large trunk." Then let your child give you the answer, which is *elephant*.

6. Now let your child think of something and give you clues.

7. Another variation of this game is to have your child get clues by asking you yes/no questions about a mystery item.

   a. "Is it large?

   b. "Does it make a loud noise?"

Treasure Hunt

This game is great for reading comprehension. It also helps your child learn how print and pictures carry meaning.

1. Read a story to your child.

2. Ensure your child is familiar with the story. You may have to read the story multiple times to your child.

3. Tell your child they are going to do a treasure hunt.

4. Find one vocabulary word, item, or character from the story.

5. If you have the item in your home, you may use it for the hunt.

6. If you don't have the item, you may draw a picture and briefly describe it on a separate piece of paper.

7. Hide the item in your home.

8. Leave a series of notes or pictures to help your child find the item. For example, write, "Go to the dining room table," or draw a picture of the dining room table. On the dining room table, have

another note ready stating, "Go to your bedroom," or draw the child's bedroom.

9. Your child will continue finding and following instructions on notes or drawings until he/she locates the item from the story.

10. Once your child has found the item, ask them to identify the item and how it fits into the story.

Charades

You will need more than one child for this game. This game is great for reading comprehension and promotes in-depth learning. In-depth learning is when you learn about something in various ways. Charades allows your child to learn words through physical activities, reading, and application (identifying where it fits in the story)

1. Read a story to your child.

2. Ensure your child is familiar with the story. You may have to read it multiple times to your child.

3. Write vocabulary words or characters from the story on index cards or paper.

4. Players will take turns picking these cards from a plastic bag and acting them out.

5. The other players will guess the word.

6. Once the word is identified, then have the child identify where the word fits in the story.

7. Another variation of this game is to have the player draw a picture of the word while the other players guess the word.

Spy a Word

1. Read a story to your child.

2. Ensure your child is familiar with the story. You may have to read it multiple times to your child.

3. Omit a word and let your child fill in the blank. Let's say you read a story where a mouse is trying to find cheese. You say, "In the story, the mouse is trying to find . . ." Let your child say "cheese."

4. Keep stating the plot of the story and let your child fill in the blanks.

5. Another variation of this game is to fill in the blanks with silly words and let your child correct you.

6. You state, "In the story, the mouse is trying to find **a cat to eat him**."

7. Let your child correct you with the word "cheese."

My husband surprised Cory by putting the Solar System in his room. He has a great view at night!

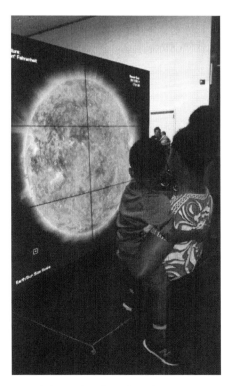

Cory and I looking at and discussing how big the sun is compared to Earth at the Air and Space Museum.

Cory identifying the planets to Daddy at the Air and Space Museum.

CHAPTER 10

Digital Media

DIGITAL MEDIA

In Chapter 5, I discussed how digital media was used to teach my son letter recognition. It is also a great resource for teaching kids how to read. Digital media should NOT be the only way to expose your child to words. It should be used to supplement your child's learning. Below I will discuss the American Academy of Pediatrics' recommendations for digital media use and how it was used to help my son with reading comprehension and learning new words.

Suggestions from the American Academy of Pediatrics

As of 2016, the American Academy of Pediatrics recommends that children younger than eighteen months should avoid the use of screen media other than video-chatting. Parents of children eighteen to twenty-four months of age who want to introduce their kids to digital media should choose high-quality programming and watch it with their children to help them understand what they are seeing.

Children two to five years should be limited to one hour per day of high-quality programs. Parents should view the program with the child and apply it to the world around them.

Other Suggestions from Experts

I remember going to the local library for a series of lectures given by a woman with a PhD in early childhood education and development. Someone from the audience asked her about toddlers and young children using a tablet, smartphone, and watching television.

She suggested that digital media be used as a supplement to what the child is learning. In other words, the child should not be introduced to a concept by these digital devices, but they can be used as reinforcement for what they already know.

I thought this was good advice, so I started reading books to Cory first and then let him watch the cartoon associated with it.

Books First

Choosing a book that has a cartoon, television show, or video connected with it allowed my son to see characters in action. These shows provided similar language written in books, and he heard the pronunciation of words we previously read. Cory likes reading Curious George books and watching the cartoons. He often becomes excited when he has read the book first and knows how it will end. He also loves when a character shows up on television that he just read about.

Sometimes Cartoon First

There are times when I don't know a book exists until my son has watched the cartoon. This has happened with the cartoons *Peg + Cat* and *Wild Kratts*. Sometimes books are created after a show has been highly viewed by children. Whenever my son likes a cartoon, I immediately research whether there is a book written about it. I find that many times there is. Usually when I get the books, my son will flip to the back and see if there are other books about the cartoon. Then he will read the titles of these books and tell me we need to get them. This is a clever way to get children to like reading, and I am all for it!

Books as a Prop

I remember watching the show *Llama Llama* on Netflix with my son and then discovering our local library has the books. The books and the episodes on Netflix followed each other word for word. While watching *Llama Llama* one day, we followed along in the book. It was great to see the ad-libbed words cartoon characters can provide to the book. My son had fun with this experience.

Enjoyment of Just Watching

Many times, you don't need the book while watching the cartoons. The joy of relaxing and viewing the television screen with popcorn is enough. It is also helpful to watch an episode that you have not read about in a book. You get to view the characters in different settings and situations from what you read. Also, this is an opportunity to be introduced to new characters that were not in the books. Children can see how their favorite characters react to new and old friends, which can lead to great discussions.

Discussions

After watching a cartoon, sometimes my son and I will discuss what we just viewed. Cory loves the PJ Masks cartoon and their books. We talked about how the villain, Night Ninja, stole the local school's sports equipment to strengthen his team of Ninjalinos. Ninjalinos are very funny characters within this storyline. We also discussed how Romeo, another villain, set up a booby trap for the PJ Masks but they tricked him into being a victim of the trap. The cartoon characters made this scenario humorous, which led us to recreate the scene through role playing.

Role Playing Based on Cartoons

Part of our playtime is reenacting books and cartoons. There are other times we will create our own story and games based on the cartoon. Let's continue with our example of PJ Masks. Cory's favorite character is Gekko, who wears green and has super lizard powers like Gekko Muscles, Super Lizard Grip, and Camouflage. Cory created a game called Gekko Solves Problems. In this game, Cory is Gekko, and I have to create problems like putting the toy dinosaur under the pillow and announcing it is stuck. Then my son uses his super Gekko powers to free the dinosaur. This game keeps my son busy for about forty-five minutes. It also keeps me on my toes, because I have to constantly create problems for my son to solve in order to keep the game going.

Books Associated with Cartoons

Below I will share with you some of the books associated with cartoons we have found. I will also share where we have watched the shows.

*Please note that most of the shows below we have seen on Amazon Prime, PBS Kids, or Netflix. Shows on Netflix tend to be temporary, so you have to search their site to see if it is still offered.

1. *Curious George* (PBS Kids)
2. *Bob the Builder* (PBS Kids)
3. *Llama Llama* (Amazon Prime)
4. *Peg + Cat* (PBS Kids)
5. *Wild Kratts* (PBS Kids)
6. *PJ Masks* (Netflix, Disney, and Amazon)
7. *Doc McStuffins* (Disney)
8. *Sesame Street* (PBS Kids)
9. *Stinky and Dirty* (Amazon Prime)
10. *Daniel Tiger* (Amazon Prime)
11. *Pinkalicious* (Amazon Prime)

12. *The Snowy Day* (Amazon Prime)

13. *Going on a Bear Hunt* (Amazon Prime)

14. *The Berenstain Bears* (Amazon Prime)

15. *Winnie the Pooh* (Amazon Prime) (Disney)

16. *Mickey Mouse* (Disney)

17. *Caillou* (PBS Kids)

18. *Arthur* (PBS Kids)

19. *Dinosaur Train* (PBS Kids)

20. *Cat in the Hat* (PBS Kids)

21. *Martha Speaks* (PBS Kids)

22. *Ready Jet Go* (PBS Kids)

23. *Maya & Miguel* (PBS Kids)

24. *Clifford the Big Red Dog* (PBS Kids)

25. *The Snowy Day* (Amazon Prime)

26. *We Are Going on a Bear Hunt* (Amazon Prime)

27. *Pete the Cat* (Amazon Prime)

28. *If You Give a Mouse a Cookie* (Amazon Prime)

29. *Clack, Clack, Moo* (Amazon Prime)

30. *Fetch! with Ruff Ruffman: Doggie Duties* (PBS Kids)

Teach Your Toddler To Read Through Play

I created a dilemma for the Gekko Solves Problems game, where superhero Black Panther needed an airplane to chase the villain Romeo. Cory, a.k.a. Gekko, built the plane and is preparing Black Panther for takeoff.

In the Gekko Solves Problems game, Night Ninja has destroyed the doctor's home. It is Gekko's job to build another home. He is on the job!

Andrea Stephenson

Oh no! Dinosaur and friends are stuck under the pillow. Gekko needs to think of a plan to free them!

ACTIVITIES

Below are other ways to use technology and media to hone your child's reading skills.

Type on the Computer

1. Let your child use a word processing program to type letters and write stories.

2. Put the font on size 18 or 20 and let them practice letter recognition or write a story.

Role-Play Your Child's Favorite Episode

1. Have your child choose their favorite episode from a cartoon.

2. Role-play this episode with your child and include props you all have created or found around your home.

Create a Villain

1. Have your child create a new villain from their favorite cartoon.

2. Create a story based on the new villain.

3. Have the child create the story using art supplies such as the following:

- Crayons
- Paint
- Paper
- Construction paper
- Other art supplies on hand

Write Fan Mail

1. Have your child write a letter to their favorite character from a cartoon they like.

2. Have the child express how much they like the character.

3. If the child can't write, then have them create artwork expressing how much they like the character. You can supplement the artwork with a written letter.

4. The child can also give suggestions for other episodes.

5. Send the letter to the company who created the character via social media, email, or mail.

CHAPTER 11

Reading a Variety of Books

VARIETY OF BOOKS

It is important to read a variety of books to your child. It exposes them to various vocabulary words, characters, plots, settings, problems, and resolutions. When Cory was a baby, I always borrowed books with the alphabet, colors, and numbers from the library. This is the main reason he knew these topics at nineteen months and could read at twenty-one months.

I also picked interactive books with colorful pictures. When reading, I would point to the characters and various objects on the page. Pop-up books are great to read to children because they create an element of surprise. It also gives them a 3-D visual of what is happening in the book.

Lift-the-flap books are great because your child is anticipating the answer to a question. They are also engaged while reading these books because they are showcasing the answers with lifting the flap. Cory has always liked to handle books; therefore, I taught him how to turn the pages at nine months. This was another strategy used to get him involved in reading as a baby.

Read Books Your Child Is Interested In

I believe children have a variety of interests, and parents can discover them through interaction, play, and observation. If children are offered reading material that follows their interests, then they will want to seek meaning from words. From this desire, they will learn word recognition and phonics skills.

Interacting and observing my son has assisted me in finding books he will connect with. I gravitate toward books with characters that look like him. Also books about cars, racing, sports, nature, animals, numbers, alphabet, and space spark his curiosity.

One day, Cory asked me how water comes into our home. This led me to get a book about how the home works called *How Does My Home Work?* by Chris Butterworth. It teaches children about items in the home that make it function, such as the circuit breaker, gas meter, and water tank. There are colorful pictures of household appliances like the dishwasher, iron, space heater, blender, and toaster. We did a hunt around our house where we found the items mentioned in the book.

Try to get books that answer your child's questions to further their understanding of a topic.

Build off of Topics Your Child Is Interested In

If Cory really likes a character or book topic, then I will use this knowledge to introduce him to other books. For example, we read a book called *What's on Your Plate* by Whitney Stewart. It teaches children about foods eaten all over the world. Cory liked this book because he found that he ate similar foods to kids all around the world. While reading about each country in the book, we located it on our globe.

After reading this book, I got more books on geography addressing the continents, oceans, etc. As a result, he learned the continents and where they are located in relation to our home continent, North America. He also learned about some of the land features.

As mentioned previously, Cory likes Curious George books and cartoons. One day we read the book, *Curious George Discovers Germs* by Erica Zappy. This book is about George the monkey learning about germs so he can figure out how to get better, stay healthy, and prevent germs from spreading to friends. This book used a colorful and humorous germ character named Toots as the villain. Cory liked it so much that I got him another book about germs and microbes called *Do Not Lick This Book* by Idan Ben-Barak and Julian Frost. It is about an oval-shaped microbe character named Min, who teaches children about germs by going on an adventure. Cory learned the word *microbe* and uses this term almost every day while brushing his teeth and washing his hands.

Trips to the Library

When Cory was between two and twenty-four months, I would take him to the library weekly for Mommy and Me programs. This program involves a librarian reading and singing songs to babies.

At the end of each program, the librarian would have a stack of books waiting for parents to check out. I always took two of the books at first; then when all the other mothers got their books, I would take what was left over. I ended up leaving with at least twenty-five books every time. It surprised me that the other mothers only took one or maybe two books. This was a great opportunity for word exposure, and it saved me time researching children's books.

If you don't have these types of programs in your area, you can still use the librarian as a resource for book suggestions. They often have lists of age-appropriate books. You can also make an appointment with them where they will teach you how to search for books on various topics.

One resource that I use at our county library is the *new book list*. Every Saturday morning at 12:30 a.m., I get an email listing all the new books the library received. I peruse through the list and put holds on books weekly that interest my son and me. This is also a major time-saver for me.

Also, if your library does not have a book you want, request that they get it or ask them to borrow it with an *interlibrary loan*. An interlibrary loan is a system in which a library borrows books from another library for the use of an individual.

Use Books to Teach Your Child New Things or to Get More Information

One day while at the science museum, we saw an enormous display of a brain and muscle in the body. I mentioned to Cory that when he smiles the brain controls this motion and the muscles allow him to do it.

We also watched the *Sid the Science Kid* episode, "Now That's Using Your Brain" (season 1 episode 40). This show explains how the brain controls many things in the body such as walking, thinking, and getting ready for school. He really liked this topic so much that we talked about it days after. He would shout, "My brain is telling my body to jump!"

Since Cory was interested in learning about the brain and muscles, I decided to get a book on the topic called *Me and My Amazing Body* by Joan Sweeney. The purpose of getting this book was to build off his interest and to teach him something new about the body, such as the lungs, heart, and bones.

This book also talked about the brain and muscles, which he knew a little about already. As a result, we have explored more about the body by putting together a skeleton puzzle and doing pretend play as a doctor where he will examine his stuffed animals' heart and lungs. He even told a pediatrician that she was going to check his heart with the stethoscope.

I continue to build upon both his and my knowledge of the body through books. Even as an adult, I learn new things with Cory!

Try Books above Their Reading Level

I remember listening to a podcast where the host was interviewing a literary expert. The expert said it is beneficial for parents to read material to children that is above their level. Children have the ability to learn the new vocabulary words and the words' context within the story. Also, children will naturally start using those words as long as the parents expose them to them repeatedly through daily discussions and interactions.

I decided to test this idea by getting the book *Big Words for Little Geniuses* by Susan and James Patterson. This book is colorful and introduces kids to big words in alphabetical order. The word for letter *A* is **ARACHIBUTYROPHOBIA!!!!** This word means "a fear of peanut butter sticking to the top of your mouth." Honestly, when I first saw that word I closed the book quickly and thought to myself, "How is this book for little kids?"

I decided to show it to my son, and we used my smartphone to look up the definition with Google, and its pronunciation with YouTube. He actually enjoyed stopping at each word and finding out more about it. We read the book a little at a time, until he was able to say all the words in the book. Go to SimplyOutrageousYouth.org and search for the post *Little Kids, Big Words – Why Not?* Here you will be able to watch the video of him pronouncing these words at 3 years old: Children's brains are amazing and can learn so much!

Another way to expose your child to books above their level is audiobooks. You can play these in the car or at home. They expose your child to stories read by professional actors and actresses. These professionals make the stories interesting by changing their voices for various characters. The music also sets the mood for the story plot. Cory learned words such as *Washington Monument* and *president* by listening to the audiobook *Arthur Meets the President: An Arthur Adventure* by Marc Brown.

Cory putting together a skeleton puzzle while learning about the bones.

ACTIVITIES

Make the Library Fun

1. On your next trip to the library, bring your child's puppets or create two puppets.
2. Use the puppets to read books to your child in the library.
3. Ensure to move the puppets' mouth while you are reading.
4. If your child can read, give them a puppet and alternate reading the pages with them.
5. Make it fun by reading in the puppets' character voice.

Get a Variety of Books

Below are suggestions for various books to read:

- Autobiographies or biographies
- How-to books
- Comic books
- Non-fiction or fact books
- Wordless books
- Alphabet or dictionary books
- Books about another culture or country
- Books about various careers
- Books about mathematical concepts such as shapes, numbers, addition, patterns, etc.

Review Parts of a Book

Please review the parts of a book while you are reading. For example, before opening the book make a note that you are viewing the front cover. Parts to take note of are as follows:

1. Front cover—note the picture, title, author, and illustrator
2. Inside the front cover where the story is usually summarized.
3. Title page—where the title, author, illustrator, copyright date, publishing company are usually given
4. Table of contents
5. Body—pages of the story
6. Inside back cover—where information is usually given by the author
7. Back cover—where reviews of the book are usually given

Make Your Own Audiobook or Video

1. Let your child create their own audiobook by reading, telling, or creating stories in a recorder or with a smartphone video.
2. If the child decides to create their own stories, below are ideas for topics. They can create stories about the following:

- A playdate with another child
- A visit from family members
- Their favorite toy
- A field trip with their class or family
- Whatever ideas they come up with

CHAPTER 12

Structuring Your Day and Game Plan

STRUCTURING YOUR DAY AND GAME PLAN

When to Expose Your Child to New Topics

It is important to expose your child to learning when they are most alert. Pick a time when their mind and body are well-rested, so they will have more energy and better concentration. The daytime is great because there is natural light and most likely their eyes will not be as tired. Additionally, ensure your child has had a nutritious meal which will fuel their brain.

On the other hand, some children prefer the evenings. In some households, the evenings are quieter with fewer distractions. Some kids retain information better just before bedtime when daytime was spent using their built-up energy on other activities.

I would like to reemphasize again: **PLEASE ensure that children are well-rested when being exposed to new material.** If not, the child will most likely be irritable and unable to focus.

Your Time and Child's Time

My advice is to take your time teaching your child how to read. This process should be natural, and the pace should be tailored to the child. Some children will pick up words faster than others. Please don't compare your child to others because they may become discouraged if someone else is moving along faster.

It can be especially difficult for children to learn when a teacher or a professional says they are behind in reading. What usually happens is that parents feel pressure to get their kid on the same level as everyone else. This pressure is then applied to the child, which in many cases results in them disliking the sight of books or reading.

It is better to start early, and I am not referring to reading, but exposing them to words and following their interests. Then they will want to seek meaning from words.

Also, if you have a daily goal to teach the child two new words and they only learn one, it is okay. Part of making this fun is having a relaxing learning environment and experience.

Remember the Learning Styles

One beneficial action to take as a parent is to learn your child's learning style. The best way to do this is through observation. Observe your child while they are playing alone, with family, and with friends. Take note of what toys they play with for the longest and shortest amount of time. Also pay attention to what makes them happy, sad, mad, and scared. This information will help in the learning process because it provides cues of when the child is ready to get up and move, sleepy, irritated, etc. It also tells you when you must adjust your lessons and activities.

Some Kids Possess More Than One Learning Style. How Do You Handle This?

As mentioned before, many kids can learn using multiple learning styles. I often use auditory, visual, and kinesthetic learning techniques with my son. The key is to find what types of activities within the learning style your child likes.

For example, within the auditory learning activities, my son enjoys audiobooks, hearing people read aloud, and listening to music. As a visual learner, he likes creating sentences with his colorful magnetic letter and using crayons and paints to draw pictures and words.

Sometimes you can use the same toy or activity with two learning styles. Let's use the Treasure Hunt game in Chapter 9 as an example. This game requires parents to choose vocabulary words from books and hide those words and/or items within the home. Then the parent will leave the child a series of notes or pictures (if they can't read) instructing them on how to find the words or items.

The Treasure Hunt game is visual because the child is seeing the item or a picture of the word in the story once it is found. You may also add colorful drawings to your written clues for visual stimulation. Make it appealing to auditory learners by reading the clues aloud to your child.

Once your child finds it, then have them tell you where it fits in the story. The fact that the words or items in the story can be touched and children are moving around the house to find them makes it a kinesthetic activity.

When you use one activity in multiple ways, you incorporate fun in-depth learning, which uses more than one way to learn. This was the best way for my son and is the best way for many children to learn.

Interaction with Children

Along with observing your children, you should interact with them on their level. Our children are constantly involved in our world, when we take them to the grocery store, to our jobs, to church, etc. It becomes their world, and this is a great thing! Children learn when they are exposed to different environments.

However, now I am asking you to be involved in their world. This means getting on the floor or sitting at the table and playing with Play-Doh or blocks. Dance around the room with your children while singing various songs. Allow yourself to be a kid again!

Only Fifteen Minutes Unless They Want to Go Longer

If you are exposing your children naturally to words, you don't need more than fifteen minutes of formal teaching a day. Other exposure could be informal, like writing out a grocery list or the dinner menu. At first, you may have to start off with five minutes and work your way up to fifteen minutes. Within those fifteen minutes, have two or three activities planned (in case your child does not like an activity), and ensure they coincide with your child's learning style. Once your child becomes accustomed to seeing words, they may choose what activity they want to do.

My husband sitting with Cory at the kids' table studying bugs in the springtime. He read about these bugs in a library book.

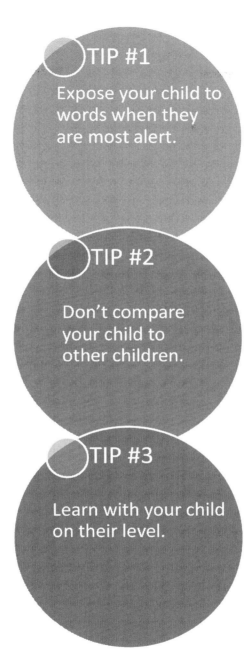

TIP #1
Expose your child to words when they are most alert.

TIP #2
Don't compare your child to other children.

TIP #3
Learn with your child on their level.

CHAPTER 13

Tips for When a Child Loses Interest in Reading

TIPS FOR WHEN A CHILD LOSES INTEREST

Pick Books that Spark your Child's Ever-Growing Interests

As children learn more and more every day, their interests will continue to grow. When Cory was a baby he loved books about farm animals. Now he is getting interested in a wider variety of animals such as sloths and skunks. One day, he asked me why people say skunks stink. This led me to get a book about skunks and how their stinky spray fends off predators. Now he requests books with skunks as the main character because he finds them funny. We have also written funny stories about skunks spraying people and their struggle to get rid of the stinky smell.

Better Yet, Let Them Choose Their Own Books

It is so much easier for my son to pick books out for himself. I usually take him to the library or the local book store and let him skim the book titles until he finds what he wants. Sometimes, he goes into the library knowing what he wants and is on a mission to find it. We find the books by inputting keywords in the computerized catalog. When we sit down to read, the first book he chooses is the one he found!

Establish a Schedule

Routines and schedules are beneficial to children because they help children understand time and time management. They also help children feel secure and comfortable because they can predict the next activity and the expectations connected with them. This decreases the frequency of behavior problems. For instance, Cory knows that after bath time, it is time to get dressed for bed and read books. He automatically calms himself and prepares to read by choosing books and putting them in a pile beside his bed.

Don't Be Overbearing—Be Natural

You don't want to be overbearing when exposing your child to reading and words. It is best to be natural. This means meeting your child where they are.

If your child wants to build with Legos, let them be creative and build what they want. In the meantime, you can describe their play by using words like *build*, *create*, *construct*, and *tower*. Also talk about the Lego colors and what they are building. Take it a step further by building letters to create words.

If you are in the store, identify letters and words on signs or advertisements. You will find that if you make it fun and natural, your child will volunteer to draw, build, hear stories, and seek meaning from words.

Other ways to be natural is to connect language to your child's interest. If your child loves princesses and is a visual learner, try drawing and coloring pictures of princesses and then writing a story or doing pretend play with your child. For example, draw a picture of a princess and write a story about how she saves her kingdom from villains.

If you have a child that loves cars, create a pretend play scenario where there is a major car race. This can be done by taking some of the child's toy cars and setting up a line where all the cars begin the race. Then you and your child race the cars. Remember to use descriptive words to describe the race, like *fast*, *slow*, *wheels*, *engine*, *mechanic*, *win*, *lose*, and *speed*.

Tip: Remember they will eventually learn to read because you are going to use *fun* in-depth learning to expose your child to words in many different ways. You may find that you have a child who loves learning new words.

Shaping

Shaping is a technique many counselors use to teach kids new behaviors. It allows you to build a desired behavior in children using small steps. Once the child has mastered a step, then you move to the next one.

This technique also requires the adult to provide a reward as the child completes each step to encourage them to go to the next task. An example of a reward could be a praise-specific statement such as, "Good job at putting all your stuffed animals in the toy box." Another example of a reward is telling a child they can play outside once a step is complete.

Shaping provides a great way to set goals as you and your child move along. Also, it requires you to adjust if you see that a child is stuck at one step. Adjusting means you may have to take a break or divide the steps into smaller increments.

Incorporate this strategy to get your children to sit and read books for long periods of time. To do so, you will start by reading a book to your child for three minutes. This means you will have to choose a short book or only read a portion of the book. Once they can sit for three minutes, then next time sit for three minutes and thirty seconds or four minutes. Keep adding on until you have reached a time in which you are satisfied. After they have accomplished one goal, provide a praise statement or allow them to do their favorite activity.

Another important point is to be patient. Some children learn new behaviors quickly, while others move a little slower.

Below Are More Tips

If your child does not like a certain activity, please adjust. This may look like the following:

- Giving them a break
- Asking them to suggest an activity
- Doing something physical like dancing or going outside to play
- Borrowing an activity from another sense or learning style
- Doing an activity that aligns with their interests

Reiterated Bonus Tip: It is important for your child to see you read books. Children pay more attention to what you do than to what you say.

When my husband is driving during road trips or long errands, my son often sees me reading a book silently. He asked me once, "Why aren't you saying any words while looking at the book?" I told him that I was reading silently. Then the next week, he started to copy me.

One night before bedtime, I saw him open the book *The Itchy Book* by Mo Willems and LeUyen Pham and stare for a while then turn to the next page. I thought he was looking at the pictures. Then I realized that he may be reading it. After he closed the book, I asked if he was reading it silently. He replied, "Yes." I asked, "What was the book about?" He said it was about dinosaurs who were itchy but they could not scratch themselves. Afterward, we read the book together, and he was right! I was proud of his reading comprehension skills!

I saw Cory building a tower for his action figures. Then we started doing pretend play with his toys and creation. He learned the words dilemma and distraction that day.

TIP #1

Choose books that interest your child.

TIP #2

Be natural in exposing your child to language.

TIP #3

Try shaping to get your child to sit and read for longer periods of time.

CHAPTER 14

What We Do Now

WHAT WE DO NOW

Continue to Read

Cory and I continue to read daily. We make weekly trips to the library and have between forty-five and fifty books checked out at one time. Sometimes, I will make trips to the library without Cory to return books and avoid late fees. I usually return ten books and borrow another ten. The librarians know us pretty well and will sometimes let us check out up to fifty-three books.

If there is a book that he really likes, I will buy it. Also, if there is a subject that he needs to know for a lifetime, like telling time, I will also purchase those types of books.

My family and friends often gift Cory with books as well. It is helpful for a child to see that gifts don't have to come in the form of just toys or clothes. This demonstrates that there is value within your circle in reading and seeking knowledge.

His Reading Level Now

Currently, Cory is three and will be four in a few months. His reading is currently on a third-grade level and maybe a little higher. He can read words such as *system*, *organic*, *disease*, *gigantic*, *performance*, and *potion* with no problems. Cory does not understand why people are amazed that he can read at his level. I think it is because he has been exposed to various words all his life and it is just natural to him. However, he does not mind the attention.

He loves to show off his reading skills. For example, whenever, he gets a greeting card from someone, he will read it to the person who gave it to him over the phone or in person in its entirety. He also loves reading signs while out and about. We have started doing science experiments at home, and he is able to follow along, read the instructions, and execute the directions.

Writing

Writing is an activity that he still enjoys as well. We have been able to write personal notes back and forth to each other since he was two and a half years old. The visual exposure to letters and words assisted him in learning to write at a young age. One of his favorite activities is to write and create his own birthday, thank-you, and Christmas cards to family and friends. I love this because it saves a lot of money!

Continue to Have a Schedule

We continuously read before bed and naptime. Other times he reads are during long road trips, bathroom time, at playtime, and if he is sitting at the kitchen dining room table while I am cooking. Because he knows the schedule so well, I often do not have to tell him to get a book; he does it automatically. It is also helpful to keep the books in designated areas around the house. This decreases distractions with finding lost books during reading time.

Still Making Connections with Words and Books

I continue to observe Cory often in his play and in the time he is just being his authentic self. This gives clues as to what topic we could read next. Currently in Sunday school at church, they are learning about baby Jesus, and I have gotten books on this subject. He also finds slime and science experiments fascinating, so I have gotten books with fun food and natural chemical science concoctions.

After children's church or swim class, I will ask Cory questions such as, "What did you do?" "What was your favorite part?" "What did you dislike?" I will get books based on these answers. For example, he told me he learned how to float on his back during one swimming session. As a result, I got a couple of books about swimming and learning new things. We also go swimming together, and I am using water and swim-related words to describe our play.

Cory loves to watch football and toss the football with his dad. He also likes watching and shooting basketball in the hoop. You guessed it! I have gotten books on both sports. As we are outside throwing and catching the football, my husband and I are using words to describe his play. We repeat words often used in football like *touchdown*, *goal*, *quarter*, *half*, and *yards*.

Another great activity we do with basketball is play the game Horse. This game involves at least two players. All players are to shoot the basketball in turns, and the person who misses a shot will get a letter from the word *horse* added to their name. The person who misses the most shots spells *horse* first and loses the game. We play this game with various words connected with basketball, such as *rebound*, *jump*, *shoot*, and *foul*. We sometimes play it with words outside basketball just to make it interesting and to learn more words.

Continue to Introduce New Subjects through Reading and Experience

I remember driving with my son and we made a sudden stop because a rabbit ran in front of the car. Both of our bodies jolted forward due to the halt. I suddenly said, "Whoa, that was *inertia*!" Cory said, "What is that?" Carefully thinking of an example he would understand, I decided to use what we just experienced. I said, "It is when your body is still moving when the car stops."

After this encounter, I found a *Sid the Science Kid* episode where they discussed inertia, and we watched it. Then we did other science experiments where inertia occurred, like stirring tea with a spoon and suddenly stopping, then watching the swirling motion continue. The next step is to get a children's book on inertia.

Reading has helped me find new subjects that interest Cory. As you know, we have read many books on various animals on a farm, zoo, and in the wild. He loves reading about their "creature powers" and what they eat. I thought he would like to learn about more animals, so I got him the book *Animal Almanac* by National Geographic. At first glance, I thought the book would be a bit overwhelming because it featured over one hundred animals. However, I was wrong. He loves this book. Cory goes to the book's index, finds an animal, and learns about them in alphabetical order.

His new interest is putting everything in alphabetical order. For example, he will take shapes and put them in order according to how they are spelled. He also likes to create stories based on order also. During bath time, he will put the letters in order and we will create stories based on their placement. For instance, the story will go something like this "Once there was an *apple* who wanted to play with the *banana*. However, the *banana* was busy playing with the *carrot*." We usually keep going until we get to *Z*.

How You Can Apply All This Information

This book has given you detailed accounts of how my son learned to read. I encourage you to follow the activities in this book. Also, observe your child and figure out how they learn best. Choose books on subjects they like, and their love of reading will grow. Once they grasp a love of seeking meaning from words, reading becomes inevitable. Have fun with this process, as kids already know how to have a good time. Thank you for reading.

Cory's bookshelf in his room. It is always full of books!

ACTIVITIES

Continue to Read

- Read to your children daily.
- Choose books that interest them.
- Let them choose books to read on their own.
- Make reading fun by incorporating the reading games from Chapter 9.
- Go to SimplyOutrageousYouth.org and do a search for the blog post *Read Aloud Strategies – How to Make Books Come Alive for Kids*

Make Connections with Words and Books

- Describe your child's play.
- Read books based on cartoons or any of their favorites.
- Read books that answer their questions and comments.
- Read books with characters they can identify with. Examples are as follows:
- Characters that resemble them.
- Characters that have the same interest.
- Characters that have a quality they want, like being fast or friendly.

Introduce New Subjects through Reading and Experience

- If you are taking a trip, get a book on the city or country or based on the activities you will do.
- If you are doing an experience activity like going to a petting zoo, get a book about this topic.
- If your child really likes a character in a story, get a book based on what problems they are solving.

FAVORITE RESOURCES

Growing Up Reading: Learning to Read through Creative Play by Jill Frankel Hauser

Think Big by Dr. Ben Carson/Cecil Murphey

Raising Black Boys by Dr. Jawanza Kunjufu

Help Your Child Learn to Read by Betty Root

30+ Games to Get Ready to Read by Toni Gould

Handbook for Raising Black Children: A Comprehensive Guide by Dr. Llaila Afrika

NEXT STEPS

STAY TUNED TO SimplyOutrageousYouth.org

We have blog posts and more courses and books coming in the future!

Go to our website and sign in to our *SOY Resource Library* for Accelerated Fun Learning Tips for Kids! It is updated frequently!

THANK YOU!

Thank you so much for investing in this book. For more information or further questions, please contact us at SimplyOutrageousYouth.org.

SIGHT WORD LIST

1. I
2. Like
3. To
4. Are
5. Do
6. Said
7. He
8. My
9. Five
10. Yellow
11. Can
12. A
13. Have
14. For
15. And
16. There
17. As
18. Me
19. Seven
20. Red
21. We
22. See

23. Is
24. You
25. What
26. Him
27. Look
28. When
29. Eight
30. Blue
31. The
32. Go
33. Play
34. This
35. Little
36. That
37. With
38. Jump
39. Your
40. White
41. At
42. In
43. Come
44. Here
45. His

46. Got

47. They

48. Went

49. Because

50. Black

51. An

52. Of

53. On

54. She

55. Two

56. Not

57. Three

58. Four

59. Out

60. Brown

61. It

62. Us

63. Be

64. Run

65. Love

66. Too

67. Six

68. Ten

69. From

70. Green

71. Up

72. By

73. Big

74. Off

75. But

76. Why

77. Where

78. Get

79. Who

80. Purple

81. No

82. Eat

83. One

84. So

85. All

86. First

87. Day

88. Away

89. Her

90. Pink

91. Yes

92. Was

93. Has

94. Saw

95. New

96. Could

97. Came

98. Then

99. Nine

Made in the USA
Columbia, SC
03 May 2019